The Dancers of Riverside Park
and Other Poems

The Dancers of Riverside Park

and Other Poems

Peggy L. Shriver

Westminster John Knox Press
LOUISVILLE
LONDON • LEIDEN

"Two Drafts on Drought" first appeared in the Editors' Choice section of The Poetry Guild's 1997 anthology, *Memories and Daydreams*.

"Starlight, Sun Bright" was written at the request of the World Association of Girl Guides and Girl Scouts and reprinted by permission.

"Earthrise" first appeared in *CrossCurrents,* Spring, 1993.

"Lines on History" is reprinted by permission from *The Christian Century,* Aug. 10–17, 1994. Subscriptions: $42/yr (36 issues), from P.O. Box 378, Mt. Morris, IL 61054 (1-800-208-4097).

"The Right to Hate" (Sept./Oct. 1999), "Chance Compassion" (Nov./Dec. 1999), and "Social Love, Social Justice" (Nov./Dec. 1999) are reprinted by permission of *Church & Society Magazine.*

"Mary, Maid of Nazareth" was commissioned by the Berkshire Institute for Theology and the Arts and was read publicly for the first time at one of its events. It is reprinted by permission.

"Occupation, Please: _____" first appeared in *Presbyterians Today*, May 2000.

Book design by Sharon Adams
Cover design by Pam Poll Graphic Design

First edition
Published by Westminster John Knox Press
Louisville, Kentucky

This book is printed on acid-free paper that meets the American National Standards Institute Z39.48 standard. ∞

PRINTED IN THE UNITED STATES OF AMERICA

01 02 03 04 05 06 07 08 09 10 — 10 9 8 7 6 5 4 3 2 1

Library of Congress Cataloging-in-Publication Data

Shriver, Peggy L.
The dancers of Riverside Park and other poems / Peggy L. Shriver—1st ed.
p. cm.
ISBN 0-664-22333-8 (pbk.)
I. Title.

PS3569.H743 D36 2001
811'.54—dc21   00-053453

May this book of poems fall into the hands of people
who crave the nourishment of poetic imagination,
for it is dedicated to them
and
to the person who feeds my own spirit
with love, joy, humor, wisdom, faith, and delight,
my husband.

Contents

Introduction

Skillful photographers attempt to frame a scene to guide the viewer's eye toward discovering relationships, perspectives, beauty, or perhaps irony. At the same time, the viewer brings knowledge and experience to the picture, so that the photographer cannot be sure that the intended message is the message received.

So it is with poetry. Poets bring our insights, images, words, and emotions to our craft. If successful, we stimulate others to bring theirs to the reading. That is what I hope I have done in this book.

My poems are mostly about ordinary, daily events of life that I have glimpsed in a personally illuminating way. But if you cannot, for example, see the huge, twisting trees of Riverside Park as dancers frozen in motion, then perhaps the poem will encourage you to find other images.

Each poem in this book is its own separate event. They were not written to form a whole, and yet they are bound together by my way of seeing, by the cumulative experience of my life. Many of the encounters are common to us all and therefore encompass universal experience. Although I wrote these poems at different stages of life than those I wrote about in my previous collection, *Pinches of Salt*, I believe that many could have been written at almost any time. A few of them are more particular and draw upon travel to different parts of the world. While the events and details may be exotic, even these poems often provide startling new images to some old themes. (See, for example, "The Johannesburg Zoo" or "To Lenin's Tomb We Stroll.")

Usually a poem has its own internal insistence, a moment to be born. Material for a poem may lie buried for years before a satisfying way of expressing it emerges. So perhaps the most difficult poems to write are those that have been commissioned for a particular occasion or circumstance. These poems have a deadline, a purpose, an expectation that the poet must honor. It is both a relief and a joy when the poetic spirit is stirred by such a challenge—but it is never a certainty! Accepting the challenge does stretch the extent of one's scope, so even the occasional disappointment is worth the risk. Poems such as "A Day-Care Center Trilogy," "Chance Compassion," or "The Vanity of Vanity" would never have been written without a request.

Grouping these poems into a few large categories is a bit like putting eels in baskets. Some could as easily slither into another basket as stay where they have been placed. But there is nevertheless a coherence to the categories that enriches the poems grouped together under each broad theme.

Cityscape, Countryside and Cosmos. Juxtaposing poems written in New York City with those composed in the Berkshire hills adds contrasting significance to the individual poems. Several travel poems also contribute unusual symbols, like the music of "Victoria Falls." Nature is a "natural" source of inspiration for poets, but the combination of visual description and personal emotional response is necessary to turn a word canvas into poetry—"Maple" and "Dramatis Personae," for example. When we observe closely, the city pulses with small dramas, as "A Collision of Cups" and "The Spirit of 34th Street" illustrate. Both city and countryside exist in the context of our expanding awareness of our place in the cosmos ("Earthrise" and "Starlight, Sun Bright").

Confrontations. Writing about injustice and social ills may result from an immediate confrontation or in response to events experienced through another's words. Travel has introduced me starkly to events of gross injustice about which I had previously only read, and the searing combination of reading and raw confrontation has incited several poems. In Germany I visited several concentration camps, Auschwitz and Buchenwald in particular, and lived for four months in Berlin on placid Lake Wannsee, just out of sight of the Wannsee conference center where details of the "final solution" of the Jews were developed. No amount of reading about the Holocaust has the impact of actually being there—but the reading is essential to understanding. While spending two months in South Africa before apartheid was ended, my husband and I visited Khayelitsha, a black township where dispossessed and dislocated people tried to survive that harsh regime. I was entering the world of Alan Paton, J. M. Coetzee, Nadine Gordimer, and Desmond Tutu! But it has not been necessary to travel abroad to face very personally such issues as homelessness, violence in city ghettoes, the dangers of war and hatred, and the need for compassion and forgiveness, to which a number of these poems attest.

Believing Is Seeing. In most of my poems I look out at the world with eyes of faith, but I do not look directly at subjects and symbols of faith itself. On occasion, however, I have used meditation on scripture, a public lecture, or the request for a commissioned poem to address matters of faith straightforwardly. Several poems grew out of an unusual request from the Berkshire Institute of Theology and the Arts to write a "modern psalm-like poem" for ecumenical worship or to write about Mary, mother of Jesus, as a Protestant steeped in the Magnificat. Rather than testify to my religious beliefs as a Christian in poetry, I prefer to invite others to explore their own convictions as I reveal the effects of my own in my responses to the world around me.

Transitions. Daily living is a constant stream of transitions—health, work, family maturation, moving, aging. Some of the darker transitions are also described in *Deep Waters*. Many transitions are occasions for joy, gratitude, humor, or appreciation—like "Opening the Summer House"—so some poems are partly serious, partly playful. Others are my way of handling disturbing events, such as losing one's job, suddenly having to spend too much time in doctors' offices, or taking on new responsibilities. One poem, "Evaluating Dreams," is the result of a new assignment as a national evaluator for the federal inner-city AmeriCorps program that works partly through the National Council of Churches. Impressed with the difficulty of working in some of the most troubled and economically stressed areas of our country and the stubborn commitment required, I added this poem to my official evaluation.

Contemplating Christmas. Each year the holiday season brings a special challenge to search deep within myself to find an authentic message. I think through the past twelve months and search for the suitable word or symbol that will focus the meaning of Christmas this time. It may mean reacting negatively to the "sweet baby" images of Jesus in an impoverished world or to the gaudy commercialism surrounding Christmas. Perhaps I find a positive message in the blue spruce "Christmas trees" outside my Berkshire window or in the onion domes of a Russian church shadowing Lenin's now neglected tomb. By November I often feel the stirrings of a new insight, an appropriate word that enriches the next Christmas.

Portrait Gallery. Edgar Lee Masters, in *Spoon River Anthology*, wrote poems about real people he knew in his community, creating believable—sometimes embarrassingly recognizable—portraits of his neighbors and associates. Although very particular, these sketches had universal appeal because they described common human characteristics. Because of the purpose of my own set of portraits of colleagues and friends, I do not dwell on foibles or weaknesses but on strengths and key qualities of characters and personal gifts. These poems were written on occasions to honor friends—as they retired, moved, or had milestone birthdays. You may not know my friends, but you will know people like them. You may even recognize something of yourself! In some instances I have identified the person with a footnote to clarify some aspect of the poem.

Deep Waters. When the death of dear friends and colleagues occurs with anguishing frequency, mortality and mourning become an inescapable reality. As I meditated on the Beatitudes, I was struck by the blessedness of those who know how to share in your mourning, who bring God's comforting spirit to you in a very direct way ("Mourning with Those Who Mourn"). In my own mourning I wrote "Legacy," which honors a woman who knew how to die gracefully as well as live generously—Margrit Suter. The death of another friend and colleague, Rev. Arie Brouwer, is explored in "The Killing Frost." His death in his prime was hard to understand, and I wrote about it sitting on the front porch of our Berkshire home, our "high ground" that is late to be touched by frost—the image I use in the poem.

Reminders of mortality, including retirement, also stimulate a search for meaning in life. Visiting places where I have spent significant moments early in life that continue to stamp my existence contribute to that search ("Circling Back to Campus"). When I left work behind in mute, stuffed office files ("An Office Stonehenge") or when I packed my possessions to move to a new residence ("The Mortal Mover"), I searched for meaning—for continuity and a sense of participation in the whole human community. Ultimately, I ask the questions raised by the author of Ecclesiastes (Are we mere dust? Does anything last? Is anything worthwhile?), and I struggle to find my own answer in "The Vanity of Vanity."

Gazing at the Sun. The most inadequate poems I write are about the great love I have found in marriage. But on my husband's seventieth birthday I tried to describe some of the special attributes of this remarkable person with whom I have daily and eagerly drunk our cup of blessing ("A Paean"). One modest wedding anniversary poem relates to his belief that he is never so loved as when he is serving me breakfast in bed ("A Breakfast Blessing"). It is almost easier to express the depths of my feeling when I contemplate his absence ("Farewell, My Love") than to gaze directly at the "sun" of blazing love ("I Cannot Bear to Look upon My Love").

Together we were invited to visit the special rare book collection of Jewish Theological Seminary's great library. Holding in my hand one of the library's treasures—the Bible of Robert and Elizabeth Browning—was a moment of pure joy. This occasion, as I remembered the immense adequacy of Elizabeth Barrett Browning's love poems to Robert, became the stimulus for my own "Testament."

The gift of marriage is hinted at, barely, in "Marriage Bounds." I acknowledge the inability of my poetic gifts to encompass all that love offers—both human and divine—in these personal love poems, but also in all my poems, for they are about life lived as the gift of a loving Creator. The desire to express my gratitude will continue to impel me to write poetry, however. If these poems encourage you to release your own poetic skills, or to discover the lens of your own eyes of faith, they will have served an even larger purpose.

Peggy Shriver

Cityscape, Countryside, and Cosmos

The Dancers of Riverside Park

The elms of Riverside
  remove their veils
    in wintertime,
While we draw close
  our cloaks against
    the river wind.

They dance bare-limbed,
  twigs splayed like hair
    against the sky.
Deep-rooted to Manhattan schist,
  their trunks thrust up
    with elemental strength.

I watch in awe
  these twisting giants
    dance in place.
Despite the clapping wind
  and my admiring eyes,
    they do not stir at all.

Like motion photographed
  these mighty elms
    communicate their joy.

A Collision of Cups

Submissive to the thunder of the rails,
the riders rest their eyes unfocused
    on the subway floor,
      refusing the assault of insolent graffiti
      that taunt their alien and alienating scrawl
    everywhere but underfoot.

As doors slide open, bawling, then muffling the subway's roar,
a blind man feels the aisle with his feet,
      extending in his hand
      a cup of meager gratitude.

Wary passengers cast their good eyes
    upon that cup,
    but no one moves to fill it.

From opposing doors another tinkling symbol clangs;
a robust youth, lacking only legs,
    lurches down the aisle,
    his cup overflowing
    from obvious need.

The captive crowd, responding to his smile
and outstretched hand,
    tenses for the pending shoot-out
    of drawn cups.

Sensing the hulk—but not the crutches—before him
the blind man shakes his cup.
Shifting his weight upon one crutch,
the boy plucks a coin
    from his own cup
    and drops it in the other.

Like loaves and fishes
the coins multiply
as passengers, abashed,
fill the blind man's cup.
    He moves slowly on,
    baffled by grace.

The Spirit of 34th Street

Doors opened with a silent scream,
    like photographs of anguish.
    The subway paused, shed cargo
      and raged on.

She lurched aboard,
    sagged into a vacant seat,
    frail weight of her gray years
      hunched with cold.

Numb fingers plucked at rags,
    drawn close against raw misery.
    Knuckles, cracked and swollen white,
      clutched into a plea for warmth.

He, dark and lithe,
    swung down the aisle,
    taut jeans dancing
      rhythmically.

With Latin grace
    he, sidling past
    her patient form,
      in one smooth gesture

disappeared through subway doors,
    leaving in her lap,
    like folded dove wings,
      his black leather gloves.

The Johannesburg Zoo
(and War Museum)

Caged, confined or tamed,
the gentle and fierce creatures of the earth
are gathered for our joy and curiosity
as they display their excellence
unwittingly before our eager eyes:
    —the python coils in lethal indolence
    —a tortoise, in its medieval armor, confidently crawls
    —a panther, whose dark sinews move with liquid tension,
        stalks imaginary prey
    —two rhinos posture, tough in horn and hide, no challenger
        but one another
    —birds preen and scream and dip within their netted tent
    —a tiger, yawning, lies upon its back, fierce claws gentling the air
    —one camel, made, it seems, from leftovers, walks with flopping humps
        and sinks upon his knees with awkward grace
    —a crocodile sleeps with saw-teeth wide agape
    —seals dive and play in watery ballet
    —baboons and mandrills lithely clamber on huge rocks,
        flash their bulbous pink posteriors,
        and laugh
    —unconcerned great elephants flap ears and trunks,
        nuzzle their young
        and occupy their turf
    —gazelles tiptoe upon the ground,
        blending their soft browns against it

We humans in our tender skins
erect museums
for our Spitfires, Messerschmitts and Churchill tanks.
Nature has bequeathed us seeming little
to defend ourselves
in this wild world
except our brains and will to dominate.

The descriptive caption on most cages
at the zoo reads,
nonetheless,
"Enemies: Man."

Baptism

Rain in the city
Courses into concrete channels,
Makes lakes at intersections,
    where impromptu athletes test
        their broad jump
    and the timid veer
        to other streets.

Water from the sky
(An unseemly inconvenience!)
Pelts the hurried crowd,
    heads ducked, collars up,
    umbrellas a pathetic shield
        against the whip of water.

Unyielding sidewalks, streets and roofs
Resist the rain and send it
Gushing down dark sewers
    to the sea,
    where water
        properly belongs.

The city, washed and scrubbed
Despite its inattention, like impatient children
Eager to return to play,
    bustles on,
    unheeding the beatitude
        of its immersion.

Rain in the country
Finds a billion thirsty mouths,
Which, until slaked,
    gulp their drink of life
    with greediness
        and joy.

Trees and bushes toss their leaves
And preen beneath the shower,
While hidden seeds
    swell and burst,
    their promises fulfilled.

When clouds depart,
The sun receives sparkling glints
From diamond-studded leaves,
        and from rich darkened soil
        thriving plants raise their heads
            in praise.

Two Drafts on Drought

(1)

My throat parched raw with empathy,
    I scan the woods for dying trees
Whose leaves are prematurely brown
    And roots sip dust while branches grasp
For air and cool, refreshing breeze.

Along the road once verdant slopes
    Are startling tawny tufted dunes,
Where grasses lost the battle for
    Each drop of dew or misty cloud
To wind and weeds and sly raccoons.

Like triage on a battlefield
    My life-supporting garden hose
Feeds dear perennials and then
    Tomatoes, beans and lettuces,
As I decide what dies or grows.

That rain should fall upon the just
    And unjust in an equal measure
I understand much better than
    This drought where only toughness wins
And god-like choices bring no pleasure.

(2)

The shallow-rooted trees
    are losing leaves
        in pre-fall fall.

Nocturnal creatures sniff
    for water under plants
        fresh set, pawed loose.

Basil droops midday,
    revives at night,
        upright at dawn.

Bird song seems subdued,
    The hummingbird
        in urgent thirst

Darts frantically to blooms
        deep-throated with
                a nectar pool.

Grass browns, then crisps
        beside the greedy green
                of warrior weeds.

Dry air casts clarity
        upon the hills
                and evening stars.

While hidden waters flow
        for those who
                drink deep.

Dramatis Personae

Pondering my life from day to day,
I gaze across our valley to the hills:

> Whose changing wardrobe may display a cloak
> of green, of bold warm hues, of winter white.

> Veils swathe the hills in solemn mystery,
> their size and number hinted, not revealed.

> Clouds seethe around a mountain's stolid base;
> it rises firmly through the smoldering roil.

> Then heavy brows descend upon the hill;
> it frowns and lowers through the steel-gray mist.

> Or puffs of powder lightly dust its face;
> a ruff of cloud is gathered at its throat.

> The hills play peek-a-boo as clouds scud past—
> a marvel of adroit transparency.

> Behind the massive profile of the hills
> an evening curtain glows in reds and gold.

> Soon smoke lifts from the heaps of mountain ash;
> in silent conflagration, day departs.

The passive hills, unwitting nature's stage,
depict conflicting dramas in myself.

I lift my eyes to mountains, sky and God
to learn my role within the universe.

Maple

A maple tree spread tall in our front yard,
 obscuring in full leaf our mountain view.
Each year we firmly vowed to cut it down,
 but *after* its fall splendor in red hue.

In winter as earth slept the tree stood guard,
 its branches patterning against the sky,
And we could see the hills so nicely framed
 that we forgot our wish to make it die.

One spring, as buds were thickening its twigs,
 we felled the maple tree as we had planned.
Branches crashed and scattered promises
 that withered heedlessly upon the land.

Today its stump clings stubbornly to soil
 among the rocks and flowers on our slope.
It sprouts a bushy spray of leafy shoots
 that burn in autumn like a ray of hope.

Victoria Falls

An elemental thunder,
　　　　ground tone,
　　　　an organum
precedes the sighting
　　　　of the misty plume,
　　　　a constant cloud
　　　　　　　above the tangled trees.

No grand pavilion,
　　　　vaulting arch or
　　　　pride of steps
leads strangers to
　　　　this crystalline cascade.
　　　　A humble path
　　　　　　　through forest bush
　　　　　　　opens on a tantalizing glimpse.

A rush of overtones,
　　　　of frequencies too high
　　　　and numerous for ear to separate
　　　　　　　commingle with the throbbing
　　　　　　　organ bass—
"Rock music" felt
　　　　within one's own
　　　　pulsating depths.

Mist gathers like our tears
　　　　as, standing in the plume
　　　　once seen afar,
we gaze upon the vast
　　　　hypnotic plunge.
　　　　The river spreads a mile across,
　　　　　　　deceptively becalmed
　　　　　　　before inevitable
　　　　　　　　　glorious descent.

We take our measure of the falls
　　　　from every viewing point,
　　　　　　　then, drowned in wonder,
　　　　　　　music, mist,
　　　　　　　　　we quietly withdraw

In memory I contemplate the falls,
    am comforted to know
    they thunder still
        without my willing
        or attending to their course.

Their splendor sings in me
    a paean of perpetual praise
    to that *mysterium tremendum*
        above, beyond, beneath,
        within us all.

Paradise Garden

(To Howard Finster, folk artist,
Summerville, Georgia)

A path of broken bits of mirrored glass
      reflects the heavens in your garden's way.
Discards and rusting junk wait in the weeds—
      perhaps potential motley sculptures, too,
Or simply bleak reminders of our clay.

The preacher in you doesn't trust your art
      to speak the gospel you mean to convey.
A hundred written messages proclaim
      the paradise your wooden angel sings,
Or warnings wrecked old battered cars portray.

Without discernment yet with deference
      you hang the offerings of folk with faith,
In hope their fierce collages will persuade,
      if not your Grandma Moses pastorals
And cheerful angels perched above a grave.

As you age toward the truth of your convictions,
      the garden paradise betrays decay.
Collectors grab the art for their safekeeping;
      your children raise the price—but also craft
Their own best visions for a latter day.

Tilted steps, the weeds, raw hammered boards
      suggest a country pastor's modest pay.
You boast a life exemplary and rich
      with promise from the God of Paradise,
Among whose treasures you already play.

The World in Black and White

Above the parting winter clouds
    I glide at lofty height,
Gazing at the snowy earth—
    The world in black and white.

The textured, sculptured, shadowed hills
    With trees brush-stroked in black
Are cold and rigidly remote,
    Bold lines that yield no slack.

Etched beauty spreads its stark relief
    In patterned clarity—
No subtleties of color here,
    No ambiguity.

This view refreshes me and yet
    Slight comfort does it bring.
I miss earth's nuanced vibrant hues
    And yearn to welcome spring.

Starlight, Sun Bright

Strange music from the stars
    sings in my heart at night.
        Perhaps you hear it, too.

The stardust in my bones
    dances to its pulse.
        Perhaps you're dancing, too.

When the waking sun
    bursts above the hills,
        I flood with amber joy.

Its arms of light embrace
    the earth along its path.
        Do you, too, gleam with joy?

The cosmic music, brilliant beams
    are messages of love.
        I dance my gratitude.

The Spirit of the universe
    enfolds both you and me.
        Let's share our gratitude!

Earthrise

Earthrise,
translucent bubble in a thick dark sea,
your skin appears so fragile it could burst
at timid touch.
Silently suspended, still, yet spinning
in deep mystery, slung around the sun
as by a brave celestial David,
You are an icon of our time.

Earthrise,
a desecrated wanderer of space,
we scrape you, dig you, mine you,
waste and plunder, bomb, pollute you.
Yet we also harvest, tend and plant you,
study, paint, extol, protect you, for
You are an icon of our time.

Earthrise,
you are the necessary gift.
Without your hospitality within the void
our spatial wanderings could only bring cold death.
Such generosity reveals our God,
whose love suffuses us like atmosphere,
as we breathe life and live our gratitude.
You are an icon of our time.

Dawning Image

Upon the velvet silence
    of our country home at dawn,
I heard a rude loud knocking
    that aroused in me a yawn.

I stirred, then nestled back
    into my dream, still unaware
of heavy steps ascending on
    our wooden spiral stair.

Up and up they pounded
    'til I woke and realized
the knocking had continued
    but no one materialized.

I grasped your hand, beloved.
    We crept down in disbelief.
(A stranger having need of us?
    A vagrant—or a thief?)

By now our earth had tilted
    toward its rising golden round.
In a mirror made of window
    that just barely touched the ground,

An angry turkey flapped
    and banged his head against the pane.
The wild old bird was battling
    with his image—all in vain.

Each time the turkey thrust
    the other bird returned in kind.
Such equality in battle
    over turf is hard to find!

In the street talk of our cities
    now a "turkey" has become
a person who is awkward, odd,
    or just a little dumb.

But I shall always see that bird,
    despite my drowsy sight,
at war with his deluded self
    in escalating spite.

I wonder if our Maker,
    looking at the human scene,
sees nation states as "turkeys"—
    just as futile and as mean.

Confrontations

A Notice in *The Times*

When his heart stopped on 42nd Street,
    the hearts of nearby shopkeepers were moved.
A crowd convened around his prostrate form,
    familiar fifteen years these city streets.
Good for greetings, sweeping up of trash,
    a lookout to detect a petty thief,
he earned his modest keep of cast-off clothes,
    of coffee, doughnuts, heat from sidewalk vents.

Respectful of his space, his neighbors smiled,
    exchanged a pleasant word, but did not ask—
beyond his need for food or change of clothes—
    where he once lived and loved and had a name.
His death exposed his anonymity
    for what it was—a life diminished by
his neighbors' disregard, excluding him
    from all but simple human interchange.

Kind gestures may betray a large neglect.
    A merchant bought a notice in *The Times*
to honor in his death this homeless man
    posthumously accorded dignity.

Another homeless man, a veteran
    of our old wars—and now of painful peace—
without a shelter, job or family,
    had burned to death from bonfires meant to warm.

A kind philosopher, a man of song,
    he'd drugged his mind but kept his heart intact.
His funeral brought state and church to mourn
    this roofless man whose life they failed to serve.

A woman in a stairwell on my street
    sits in shadows deepened by despair.
Eclectic clothing layers her worn flesh.
    She, too, lacks home and ordered dignity.

Discomfort floods me as I sense through her
    the homelessness of dreams denied, hope lost.
Why must her *death* teach us to see her whole,
    whom God intends to love through you or me?

Lines on History

Lines of broken people
    staggering along a path that races from,
        not toward, their burning homes,

Faces drained of hope and energy,
    eyes numb in blank refusal
        to recall the horrors they have seen,

They drag themselves, their cringing children,
    vacant-faced or terror etched,
        driven, not drawn, along an unknown road.

Miles of lines,

        lines,

    lines,

        lines,
Meandering like a river.

Lines of buoyant people,
    prancing along a path to polling booths,
        toward dignity and nationhood,

Faces flushed with hope and energy,
    eyes brimming tears of incandescent joy
        that lights the shadows of a pain-wracked past,

They dance the *toyi-toyi*, children held aloft,
    singing as they wait in patient purpose
        to cast themselves upon an unknown road.

Miles of lines,

        lines,

    lines,

        lines,
Deep flowing like a river.

Rwanda and South Africa—O God of history,
Are these lines drawn by you?
Are they streams of one river?
    I do not know.
I only know Christ stumbles along one,
    and dances in the other.

War's Gulf

While sitting peacefully
    in my own home,
and scraping up the leavings
    from my plate,
I watch the daily news
    and witness death.

I'm looking through a bomb-sight
    at a tank
ensnared in laser cross-hairs
    on my screen.
I stare, immobile,
    as it flares below.

How dare they implicate me
    in their war
or make me a voyeur
    of violence!
Imagination balks;
    I shut my eyes.

But shutting eyes makes me
    play Pilate, too
(a role that even he
    did not perfect),
which warfare televised
    makes obsolete.

Millions see the kill,
    but no one hears
the suffocating gasps,
    the searing screams.
I pray that Christ
    be in their sufferings:

Sparing them—and also
    sparing me.

The Right to Hate

When someone wronged,
    yes, deeply wronged my child,
I felt the rage of hatred
    scorch my soul.
Left weak and wasted,
    angry, seething, wild,
I tasted bile,
    its acid eating me.
Shocked, I learned
    my own desire to maim,
To devastate, destroy
    my enemy.
Lurking in my body's
    civil frame,
Some untamed, vile
    and vengeful spirits dwell.
Uncorked, they could contaminate
    the whole
And make my life—
    and yours—a constant hell.

I've seen them
    in the jeering, sneering band
That spat upon a black girl,
    brave and mild.
And in rampaging mobs
    that trample hopes,
Where hatred has de-faced
    humanity.

For hatred, a volcano, can erupt—
    Like spewing fire and ash into the air,
    Slathering lava down its heaving slopes
    Until its glistering cone is seared and bare—
And hatred the avenger will corrupt.

When wronged, I justify my right to hate
And wrong myself with double injury
By putting into my opponent's hand
The weapon certain to demolish me.

Chance Compassion

Samaritans of virtuous intent,
We take the side of robbers through neglect
If we should fail the road toward Jericho
To guard, police, or frequently inspect.

For other hapless travelers may soon
Fall victim to the robbers' evil greed.
Then our concern and love depend upon
Our strolling by at just their time of need.

Social Love, Social Justice

...The crafty arts of politics
...Arcane theories of economic justice
...Strategies of controlled violence to control violence
...Imperfect love that festers into hate
...Preservation of an earth we nurture—and destroy

Perhaps we ought not bother God
About each messy deed,
Our sin-soaked public policies
And wily webs of greed.

God has lived among us, knows
Us individually—
How easily we justify
Injustice socially.

But God, who Christ has promised loves
Us jointly and apart,
Commands we also do the same
With glad and contrite heart.

That is why throughout the years
Our church will undertake
Ambitious and ambiguous tasks,
Our mutual love at stake.

This powerful, expansive God
Of universe and space,
Despite conniving selfishness,
Still loves the human race!

River in the Desert

(on Isaiah 43:20)

From opposite horizons
Bands of people roam
Upon the desert sand,
    barren, raw, and hot.
    Angry winds have roiled
    the landscape into dunes.

Each shuffling band
Approaches warily
    its militant mirage.
    Fists rise and shake.
    They pantomime
    long-practiced rage.
Close enough at last
To voice their hate,
    they howl fresh pain
    at one another,
    grievances and wrongs
    still documented
    in their flesh.

Hoarse and worn,
They slowly lower arms
    and raise their eyes,
    reading terror, misery, abuse,
    but—most of all—humanity
    in one another's face.
Each listens to harsh tales
    of anguish, loss, remorse.
    Tears flow into the sand.

Their weeping greens the soil,
Spreading an oasis
    of forbearing hope
    that one day these
    nomadic enemies
    might pitch their tents
    beneath a tree
        of true community.

Auschwitz—in Concert

(Berlin Memorial Concert, 1995)

Once again we try
    to wring appropriate grief
    and anguish from ourselves,
As Jews cite new brutalities
    that stir chaotic memory
    throbbing through our veins.
We gray heads, seemingly impassive,
    row on row in this gilt hall,
    listen to these men—
Master accusers
    to the master race
    of humanity's most systematic crimes.

We try in music, poems, art,
    in rhetoric and prayer,
    in drama, photos, dance
To comprehend our evil acts.
    There are not tears enough,
    nor penitential rage,

Nor rituals of mourning
    to face the demon in ourselves
    and wash our stains away.

We count therefore
    on God to pry apart
    our chasm walls clamped shut
Against the ugly truth
    God knows is buried there.
    For God prepared a Jew
To brave those depths
    and claim the power
    to transform.

Wannsee Vertigo

(Berlin, 1999)

Across this placid lake
The "Wannsee Conference"
Of sharply uniformed
And jolly, cocky Deutch
Gathered one fine day
In camaraderie
And finalized their plans
To manufacture death
With grim efficiency,
Accommodating all
Who failed to meet their test
Of full humanity.

My eyes transfix upon
This lovely, horrid scene
With anxious vertigo.

An evil of this evil
Is its protean disguise
As calm and beautiful.

Flotilla on the Flats

Shreds of plastic snag on wired fence
Like tattered banners heralding approach.
Streams of people walk the new-paved road
With burdens on their heads—and some within.
A tilted bus, exhausted, lumbers past.
A few lone frontier shacks rise from the ditch
On either side the modern highway's rim,
Most recent of the mass of dispossessed
Whose numbers from the homelands daily mount
And press against the city with their need.

Their patchwork huts of cardboard, plastic, wood,
Are monuments to ingenuity,
To suffering, to self-assertive will,
To disillusion with the white man's dream
Of severed peoples in a distant home.
Now thousands upon thousands of these shacks
Crowd and squat upon the treeless flats.

Within this squalid, stark community
Tall graceless polls point searching lights
That beam upon a million miseries.
But shadows hide the raging violence
That, once unleashed, can hack and burn and kill
Whatever lies within its radius.

A rise of highway lifts my anguished gaze
To glimpse the vast flotilla on the flats,
At last acknowledged by authorities
Through highway signs in simple green and white:
KHAYELITSHA.

Khayelitsha is a South African township just outside Cape Town. It grew rapidly through a continual arrival of squatters from destitute homelands—the result of South Africa's disastrous apartheid policy, a policy abolished soon after this poem was written.

Shanghaied

A cloudburst of wealth
Rains upon Shanghai,
Leaving skyscrapers
Piled high like coins,
Towers of Babel
Clawing upward
As far as one can see.

Gone the stranger's dream
Of smiling roofs,
Fabled tranquil gardens
Bathed in jasmine scent,
Shy maidens delicately
Offering a cup of tea
Upon a lacquered tray,
While pentatonic melodies
Echo through the mists.

Shanghai has been Shanghaied
By gold or opiate of steel,
Jackhammers pounding
Through the night,
High clicking heels,
Sirens, horns,
Hard metal rock,
Amid pollution's haze.

Inland, on Western slopes
In meager villages
Other Chinese scan
The far horizon
For dream clouds, too,
Perhaps seeing just
A gathering storm.

D'yaknowwhatI'msayin'?

Shifting sneakered feet,
He scans his audience
And hitches up his jeans.
Cornrows cross his brow.
Deep-furrowed, dusky skin
Frames a broad, shy smile.

He tells a tale of guns,
Of drugs and gangs and pride.
D'yaknowwhatI'msayin'?
A bullet in his back,
His mother, brother killed
By rivals dealing drugs,
He looks through all of us
And links his thoughts again—
D'yaseewhatI'msayin'?

He's really still a boy
But older than most men
In pain and fear and grief.
Know what I'm sayin'?
A father, too, he is,
And hopes to raise his child,
Though jail has intervened.
D'yaknowwhatI'msayin'?
He's taut between two dreams—
One, nightmare; one, a hope,
Pale light before the dawn.
See what I'm sayin'?

The streets have shaped his speech.
His words rap a tattoo:
D'ya-know-what-I'm-say-in'?
At first it interferes,
Affected, filling time,
But as he sits, that phrase
Drums on in urgency:
D'YA KNOW WHAT I'M SAYIN'?

Re-Union

The strong Montana mountains of my youth
    uplift me to a canopy of sky,
    where I can sense the spaciousness of God.

Last year I gave myself to ministry,
    began the sober discipline of school
    and left my hills in fearful hope and joy
    to live among the people of the world
        amassed in New York City like the rocks
        on mountain slopes of my beloved home.

Some people near my school were hungry, lost,
    bereft or homeless, so I offered food
    and friendship through a caring Broadway church.

But buildings of the city, tall and proud,
    leaned against my spirit, closed my sky.
I eagerly returned to hills and home.

Yet in the fall, reluctantly I trod
the shadowed canyons of the city streets,
    alone, afraid, unsure that I belonged.

A cluttered Broadway stretched before my eyes.
Then half a city block away I saw
    a figure with a welcome wave and smile
    gleaming from a dark familiar face.
    Wide arms embraced, enclosed this prodigal.

    "Hey, man! I missed you. Where you been?
    I'm glad you're back, Bill. Feared you might not come."

Suddenly, the spaciousness of God
    expanded me—and humbly I rejoiced.
    A homeless man had given *me* a home.

A student at Union Theological Seminary in New York told me about this incident.

Crowd Control

(Central Park Peace Rally, 1982)

We have been awash in many crowds—
    like Macy's—where the surge and crush
    are engined by impatience, greed
        or curiosity.

Going everywhere, the crowd goes nowhere,
    each part imprisoned by the rest,
    edges pressing in, compacted by confusion,
        raising tempers,
        slowing tempo of the mass.

But one crowd with which we joined our feet
    and hearts had but one mind—
    to demonstrate against the mushroom cloud
        that spews out spores of death.

Like tributaries of a lake pooled toward its depth,
    the human streams flowed from the avenues
    to Central Park's Great Meadow
        as policemen nodded, smiled, their nightsticks
        peaceful at their sides.

When children lagged, their fathers hoisted them
    upon strong shoulders, as if
    to lift them to a safer world.
        Old couples, hand in hand, let others pass,
        still moving to the music of the march.

Comrade groups (just friends, not communists)
    displayed their camaraderie, sang tunes
    picked up and passed along the line of march
        like energy transmitted through
        a row of swinging balls.

Hawkers offered buttons, leaflets, flags
    or ice cold drinks. The day was warm and bright.
    A great vast picnic spread upon the ground.
        Banners quickly scrawled or neatly stitched
        announced arrivals from Virginia, Vermont.

A few odd opportunists cast their nets
　　into this hopeful human current.
　　("Buy tarot cards here ... ")
　　　　　We wove our fingers as the lake became an ocean,
　　　　　heaving waves of eager yearning, hope for peace.

This one day of brimming love made dreams
　　Seem timid
　　　　　And real life bold.

An Easter Passion

(Easter, 1995)

"It doesn't get any better than this"
    smirks the television ad.
I lie abed, nested like a robin's egg
    with my beloved.
Coffee and fresh fruit perfume the air;
    fire crackles in the grate.
Bach's passion sounds, intensifies our own,
    while spring swells cold, damp earth outdoors.

Down the city street lie five young men
    across a hot air vent—like frankfurters.
Sharp air of early spring nips at
    their cracked and swollen feet.
Fumes of trucks and stench from
    plastic garbage bags
And traffic whine accompany their sleep.

Oh God, it must get better than this!

A Hunger for Righteousness

For Germany, no Holocaust
Americans, no slavery
Japanese, no greed for space
No Russian gulags or pogroms
Nor Chinese prison labor camps
Rwandans no mad massacres
Nor Turks against Armenians
Cambodia without Pol Pot
No Indian religious wars
Or Balkan never-ending strife
No Argentina "disappeared"
No starving North Koreans
Bangladesh, Somalians
No Latin death squads, SS troops
No missiles aimed to launch assault.

Could we expunge our history,
Back up, begin again
Before the Inquisition,
Roman Conquest
Or Crusades?
Before Spain's lusty search for gold
Upon an alien coast,
Before the Czars or Stalin,
Alexander,
Genghis Khan?

We hunger, thirst for righteousness.
But eating evil, we confess
"There is no health in us."

Oh God of grace and mercy,
When shall we be filled?

In Media Res

(A Psalmic Prayer)

The airwaves are dense with babble.
We stop our ears with sound.
Our glutton eyes imbibe the images
    we have made of ourselves.
We dance and preen,
Laugh without joy,
As we behold ourselves on lighted screens
    with rapt fascination.
We divert ourselves from God's glory.

Our images are flat, O God.
Your Spirit is not in them.
Our voices are vulgar and shrill,
    dulling our ears to your words.
Our screens are crowded with strangers.
We cry out in loneliness and fear,
    "Where are you, God?
    Can you hear us?
Do you know who we are?
    for we do not know ourselves."

Open our hearts to your presence.
Bless us that we may bless you.
Deepen the silence within us
    until we can hear your voice,
    and acknowledge our hunger.
We are starved on false food,
    the food of our self-adulation.
Renew in us hope in the holy.
We bow down before you, O God,
    and rise up to find you
        in one another.

Body Language

I'm told my body talks
but I can't listen in
as genes communicate
their "mission possible"
to one another,
like a silent Internet
of e-mail messages
for which I have no password.
My cells communicate
their urgent need
for rescue or repair.
Protean stem cells rush
to do their magic mimicry,
becoming what they must become
to make me whole again.

I am not in control
of this community of cells
that is my body.
I'm glad such diligence
on my behalf occurs
without my clumsy supervision.
For what I can do, I do not,
and what I ought not do, I do
for my own health.

Some people say
the word is out:
The secret of creation is revealed.
We've cracked the code,
can now take charge
of our own future,
thank you, God.

But I say,
let my body run itself
with only minor interference
from my personhood,
or small assist from science
and some caring hands.
I'm quite content to give to God the glory
and concentrate on living out my story.

Believing Is Seeing

A Psalm of Preparation
(A Call to Worship)

Hear us in the morning as we greet the day, O Lord.
We are surrounded by ripening fields;
Our gardens quicken toward harvest,
Blossoms sweeten the air,
And the hills dance with green veils
Of swaying trees.
We praise you for a world so beautiful
We cannot encompass it,
For a world you embrace
With your spirit and uphold
With your love.

Be with us in this sacred hour.
Let us breathe deeply the air
Of your presence.
Lift us out of our callous misuse
Of this earth and of one another.
Make us fresh and new,
Full of promise and hope, O God,
Like seed unfurling tendrils of green
From dank soil.
Drive away the preoccupations
And pressures that burden us.

Listen to our prayers of praise
For we trust in you
To make us worthy through your love
To utter them.

Amen.

A Psalmic Grace

Source of our life and hope,
our God, who has set this table before us,
we thank you for your unfailing sustenance
of our lives.
We do not always ask you
for what you choose to give us.
We sometimes take
that which you intend for others.
Receive our feeble gratitude
and multiply it with your mercy,
so that our cup runs over
with blessings on this food.

                                    Amen

There Is a Fire in Faith

There is a fire in faith.
It illuminates and purifies,
          refines, transforms,
                    consoles.

There is a fire in faith.
It rages uncontrollably,
          consumes, disrupts,
                    destroys.

There is a fire in faith,
A mystery ignited by
          the universe
                    of stars;
An inner incandescence
          stirring love and joy
                    and hope.

Approach such faith with caution
In believers that you meet,
For you cannot know its power
Until you feel its heat.

Soft as the Rock

(A Laying on of Hands)

*"You are Peter, the Rock,
upon which I build my church."*

I look at my soft hands,
    uncalloused, contemplate
the pebbles I can grasp
    to build Christ's church.

Widow's mites, these hands,
    but also bearers of perfume
to lavish, like the Magdalene,
    upon his toughened feet.

Lamp bearers, too, my hands,
    to light the Master's path,
dispel the darkness, lead
    a stranger to the light.

They sweep and clean, my hands,
    and gather mustard seed
like coin, and fold in secret
    prayer and praise.

Servants of the Lord, these hands
    perform upbuilding acts
of love when Spirit-led,
    and joined with yours.

Parabolic Mercy

"And who is my neighbor?" he asked him to test
    the wit of the teacher, his knowledge of law—
for a lawyer asked questions and others confessed.
    But Jesus' response filled his hearers with awe.

"A man on a journey to Jericho fell
    among thieves who attacked him and left him for dead."
(Jesus proceeded this story to tell.)
    Who cannot imagine yourself in his stead?

But few would identify robbers as kin,
    for often our stealing is subtle, remote.
Against generations or nations we sin.
    No bandit or murderous thug gets our vote!

But what of the Levite and priest? To their shame
    they abandoned this man in the road as they walked.
Perhaps they, like us, are not really to blame.
    Urgent affairs called them—that's why they balked.

Why a Samaritan helping a Jew?
    He must have had money and skill to impart.
I wish I could do all the things he could do,
    although he might only have had a kind heart.

But even his mercy seems quite overdone.
    His promise to pay puts him out on a limb.
Of course, were I beaten I'd want him to come
    and do unto me as I'd *like* to—to him.

A Spirited Debate

Pundits claim this year
    the word on everybody's lips
        is "soul,"

While others now predict
    the word that sells
        is "angel."

Want to promote a book, a car,
    a cereal, or soap?
        a movie, TV show,
        a Broadway play?

Then use these words,
    perhaps the two conjoined—
        a mantra
        for a sick society.

Should we rejoice that we perceive
    at least our nakedness
        of spirit?

Or fear that, so impoverished, we'll sell
    what we still quaintly call
        our "soul"?

It is a year for hucksters—
    and for God.

Altered Ego

Some of us slip gently into faith.
We hardly sense our bending into shape—
      that quiet conformation
      to the One
            who teaches love, respect and reverence
            for life, for earth
                  and all its sustenance,
            for victims, for the poor,
                the weak, the old,
            as well as for the beautiful
            and strong.

Others struggle for autonomy,
Resisting faith with will and intellect.
      They sense that to believe
      in Jesus' God
            requires a wrenching new identity,
            a new location in society,
            a life engaging it
                by altered rules.

We learn we do not fit into a world
Of grasping hands and walls of privilege,
      of mockery toward those
      who lack the force,
            the wealth and means,
            the egocentric goal
            to bend earth's creatures
                to their selfish will.

Therefore we know that we must choose to change
Or live as altered egos—
      and praise God.

Cathedral

The blank, filmed eyes
Of dark cathedral windows
Stare outside,
As though thinking
Deep within of beauty
Glowing there.

The passing world stares back,
Such beauty unsuspected,
Unless, beckoned by bells,
Summoned by spires,
Lured by opened door,
Or led by neighbor's hand,
They enter.

Within, the windows' eyes
Glow with glory,
Transmuting
Common daylight
Of the streets
Into messages of love and joy
Toward all who enter in.

A Sunday in Hangzhou

Herded down a narrow, cramped dirt street,
 Whose doorways breathe faint odors
 Of cooked eels, sea cucumbers and kelp,
Through heavy wooden doors thrown open wide,
 As welcoming as ushers' eager smiles,
We round-eyed Christian strangers,
 Dangling cameras freshly stocked,
 Lope down the center aisle,
 Past a hundred pair of curious eyes,
 While voices raise a Chinese hymn.

Bowed into front seats, we face a feeble man,
 Face carved by cares into a thousand cuts.
He clutches a worn pillow for his bench
 And shoos us stubbornly away
 From his accustomed seat,
 Despite embarrassed pleas for protocol.

Others offer hymnbooks graciously, and so
 Our mouths shape sounds our minds reject,
 Except the one word, "Hallelujah!"
Guided by familiar liturgies, we ease
 Into a time of prayer and praise
 And an English sermon, which translates
Into belated smiles on women in the choir.

Touch replaces useless tongues as,
 Patting, clasping, pointing, stroking cheeks,
 We greet, less strangers than before.
An elder hosts with strawberries and tea,
 And stories of their trials of faith.
 His gentle warmth and kindly face
 Assure us Christ still lives
 In beautiful Hangzhou.

One woman, old and frail, enacts a Pentecost.
 Pulling from her faded memory
 A precious store of words
 Held fast for such a time as this,
She trembles into speech:
 "Welcome in the name of Jesus Christ.
 God bless you!"
Yes, indeed.

Mary, Maid of Nazareth
(A Modern Magnificat)

Mary, faithful maid of Nazareth
    did your own wonder grow with motherhood,
    as life expanded in your novice womb,
    your body strangely wise in shaping it?

Mary, did you marvel at his birth,
    when nature's forces gathered in yourself
    you didn't know your body had to thrust
    that helpless, sacred child into the world?

Then, Mary, did you sense your helplessness
    when little Jesus left your sheltering arms
    and what he learned and spoke astounded you,
    as in your heart you pondered all of it?

Mary, when in manhood he did deeds
    you surely could not fully comprehend
    did you not call upon your God in hope
    for wisdom and a faithful clarity?

Mary, when he gave his life in death
    did you not wail in torment, grieve your loss
    and plead with heaven for an answer
    to your agonizing faith-filled "Why"?

Like you, dear Mary, all we mothers find
    surprising wisdom in our quiet wombs,
    feel the urgent miracle of birth,
    learn the strength and grief of mother-love.

Mary, God had need of womankind
    to enter life like all humanity,
    chastising those who try to live as gods,
    exalting those who fear and love the Lord.

Please, mother-maid of Nazareth,
    remove the halo pressed upon your head,
    exalt your sisters scorned in low degree
    and claim all women, like you, truly blessed.

Transitions

Waiting for the Holy Office

Conscious of our bodies,
we sit, uneasy,
in the doctors' waiting room,
thumbing unfamiliar magazines
while listening to ourselves
stay alive.

First things first,
we've filled out forms,
displayed our cards,
and tried to satisfy
the bustling,
healthy
office staff.

Someone groans, another sighs—
as much from over-waiting
as from overweight.
Each eyes the other,
noting symptoms, wondering,
on a scale of one to ten,
who ranks most worthy
of the doctors' time—
a silent triage, or
a wordless prayer
of thanks.

Behind closed doors
doctors welcome one by one
each anxious face,
hiding their fear
of being tested
for divinity
by every urgent, hopeful
Doubting Thomas
that appears.

Occupation, Please: _____

This gaping blank in forms,
bureaucracy's chief coin,
unnerves the unemployed,
    whose "occupation" is
    to be preoccupied
    with loss of self defined
       in monetary terms.

Who do I say I am?
(So malleable the self
to fit descriptive cores
    of worth—in paycheck earned,
    in title, benefits,
    prerogatives and roles,
    in privilege and power
    or sweat and time-clocked toil).

Who do I say I am?
Did Eve and Adam claim
they were defined by work
    before their fall from grace?

My occupation is
    to be a human self
    in awesome plenitude,
    for I am not my work.
    Before my work I am.
    Though work be killed, I live.

Who do you say I am?

Opening the Summer House

When the weathered door creaks open wide,
    We gulp the still, cool air so dense
With nutrients of rugs and wood and hearth,
    Blindfolded we would know this redolence.

Two coffee cups, washed hurriedly, rest dry
    Beside the sink with stiff and faded rag.
The kitchen, oddly clutterless and clean,
    Displays each stain and scratch or dent and snag.

Two stalks of lavish blue delphinium,
    Token of a thousand garden joys,
Retain crisp, fragile blooms upon dry stems
    Until a dusty sneeze disturbs their poise.

With eyes like guests we see the wear of time.
    A playful draft spat ashes through the vent.
But in the grate dead twigs await our match.
    Familiarity soon breeds content.

The blinking clock beneath a vacant screen,
    Signaling distress when power drains,
Appropriately reports time in suspense,
    Till we begin to reckon it again.

By setting dials, flipping switches, lighting fires
    We make our lazy Lazarus to glow.
Is this a "many mansion" of our Lord?
    If so, our heaven is closer than we know!

An eloquence has gathered in this house.
    It speaks, without employing reason's word,
The love, the peace, the glory of this place,
    A harmony in life too rarely heard.

A Gift of Blessing

I have not lost a child to violence
      (though losing takes so many forms today).
Nor am I wracked by illness, worn by pain,
      nor haunted by the ghosts of poverty.
So little suffering attends my life
      that I am poorly schooled in empathy.
My own beloved fills my heart with bliss.
      I offer thanks for daily ecstasy.

Sometimes my joy is clouded with unease,
      because I am so happy with my lot,
while others live in pain or deep despair,
      some destitute, bereft, or seared with grief.
Should I rejoice and let my candle gleam
      or snuff it out and join the gathered dark?
Yet darkness can't dispel another's gloom!
      I know some tragedy awaits us all.
The highest joy might bring the deepest loss.
      But surely God intends today's delight
as gift, as love, as promissory hope.
      So I shall bless as I am amply blessed,
assured that Christ rejoices with me, too.

Liberation Number Two

"Christ Jesus . . . emptied himself, taking the form of a servant."
(Philippians 2:7 RSV)

I am a traveler these days.
    My bag and briefcase signify
        real business, self-importance,
            value in my work.

Housewife, yes, and mother, too,
    I still do laundry, dishes,
        pick up random droppings
            of other people's lives.

But traveling by air, my head
    grazes the soft clouds, my feet
        lose touch with earth, my hands
            pick coffee off a tray.

At destination's end I struggle
    with my bag down airplane steps.
        Suddenly it lightens, moves ahead,
            swooped up by helpful hands.

I glance with gratitude to see
    this voluntary servant hoist
        my baggage handily,
            a grin on his dark face.

I recognize a civic personage,
    a banker who grew tall
        from roots sunk deep
            in Black communal soil.

He tips his hat, salutes and strides away,
    his body swaying freely,
        confidently liberated from
            a porter's cap, the cotton bale.

I stoop to gather up my bag,
    the laundry, children's toys,
        a dirty dish, all with
            a lightened heart.

If he is free to serve, then so am I.

Fabrication

(The Terrors of Public Speaking)

Arms weaving tapestry
>with warp and woof of words,
>>the speaker spreads his thoughts
before an audience
>that claps and claps,
>>saluting his whole cloth
set sail across
>a sea of smiles.

Glass in hand,
>mincing words and canapes,
>>they mingle, chattering,
to pick and peck and pull
>the threads of speech,
>>untie the knots,
until the fabric
>is in tatters.

Each hearer takes
>a tuft of thought,
>>some threads and bits
to tuck into their own
>prefabricated world
>>of shaped ideas
and builds with them
>a comfortable nest.

Travel Time

On any day I travel I awake,
    Head ticking like a metered taxicab,
As every errand, call or step I take
    Is measured from the time I walk on board
The airplane, bus or train I'm bound to make.

But once I settle down into my seat,
    The ticking meter stops within my head.
I "listen to another drummer's beat"
    And wait and wait and wait until I feel
Impatience drive the tapping of my feet.

If all of life by scheduled stops were played,
    I'd try to be forever poised and calm,
But hurry when the timetable displayed
    A need to rush. Yet realism warns
I'd only find a posted sign: "Delayed."

A Moving Thought

I envy the turtle and snail,
      who carry their house on their back—
no agonized sorting of goods,
      or endless brown boxes to pack.

I envy the nautilus, too.
      He simply adds rooms to his shell
when quarters become overstuffed
      as he moves with the ocean's deep swell.

I wish I had courage to give
      all my goods to the hungry and poor,
take your hand, my beloved, and leave—
      no regrets, just a firmly closed door.

But I know that wherever we move
      I'll acquire what I thought I had lost,
familiar and loved things replaced
      by the new—at a terrible cost!

Haiku on Becoming Forty

Forty is a surfer
Riding toward shore
    Upon the crest of a wave.

Haiku at the Beach

Sandpipers dart and peck
In jerky haste
    Like tiny Charlie Chaplins.

Travelogue

What have I seen?
    The earth, the sky
    People who eat, people who die
    Laughter and sadness, joy and pain
    People who prosper, fortunes that wane
    The best and the worst of human deed
    Beauty and ugliness, love and greed
    Praises and prayers, cries of the soul
    Broken, defiant, healed and made whole

We differ in culture, appearance and speech,
Politics, faith, technological reach,
Economics and climate and natural gifts,
Causing among us some violent rifts.

Profoundly alike but equally odd,
May we humans unite in the mind of God.

Evaluating Dreams

Despite the noisy clash of needs,
    A lack of funds, so much to do,
We still have learned to state our goals
    And measurable objectives, too.

They march across computer sheets
    Like ledgered columns in a bank
Or soldiers on maneuvers who
    Assemble into ordered rank.

So, quickly, with a practiced glance
    We scan the gains and shortfalls here.
Our crises, tensions, muddled plans
    Reorient, our purpose clear.

Evaluation offers hope
    That we *can* do what we dare claim,
Despite discouragement, despair
    Or sly distractions from our aim.

We need to mark these little steps
    Along a tortured upward climb
That seems impossible amidst
    The poverty, disease, and crime.

Yet numbers may not be precise.
    One child who never learned to smile
May more than twenty boisterous youth
    Pose a challenge to beguile.

We can describe what we attempt
    In neat, achievable fine schemes
But in our hearts we wildly yearn
    For miracles to stoke our dreams:

We glimpse a woman, spirit-bent,
    Blossom in a new vocation,
A child unlock his will to learn
    When nurtured in a calm location.

Communities begin to form
    As leaders listen, neighbors share.
Streets are bustling, clean and safe
    And gardens flourish everywhere.

Such dreams can help us persevere.
    The numbers, goals bring clarity.
Our very limits may evoke
    Evaluation's charity.

Thus we continue day by day,
    Enabled by the skills we hone,
Empowered by the joyful truth
    That we are working not alone.

We need our neighbors, staff colleagues,
    Community coworkers, friends,
And God's compassionate support
    As "to the least" we make amends.

A Day-Care Center Trilogy

When first I brought him to the day-care door,
My four-year-old sprung loose his pent-up rage
As I let go his hand and waved good-bye.
His face was purple, eyes scrunched tight and wild,
As bestial sounds roared from his mammoth cave
And fists and feet beat drum-like on the floor.

With guilty stealth I slithered out of sight,
While teacher firmly shut the day-care door
Against my abdication—and release.
When I returned, refreshed and calm, I smiled.
The door was barricaded still against
Assault from my aggrieved and angry wight.

So carefully I crept into the hall
Where many children were engrossed in play.
My son was loading blocks into a truck
And dumping them before another child,
Who topped a wobbly tower with one more.
They laughed to see their mighty tower fall.

I crouched beside and gently called his name.
My son ignored my presence and my voice
For want of which his tantrum had been spent
In vain. Perhaps he was not reconciled.
Was this cold welcome cruel punishment,
Reverse abandonment—was that his game?

Perhaps. But possibly, portentously
My child was simply happy, satisfied.

If your house were burning down
    and you could only save a few
of your most dear and precious things,
    would you forget a child or two?

Or in the story of your life
    would your sons and daughters be
simply added by your scribe
    as grace-notes to your melody?

Or is the grace of parenthood
a gift that seems unmerited,
a blessing on your wisest hopes,
a love that you inherited?

Children's Chorus: WHY?*

Always tell the truth. Avoid all lies.

Children: WHY?

Give help to little children half your size.

WHY?

Comfort and assist someone who cries.

WHY?

Look at all new things. Use well your eyes.

WHY?

Say "thank yous," "pleases," "welcomes," and "good-byes."

WHY?

Listen to your teachers, who are wise.

WHY?

Take care of toys, equipment and supplies.

WHY?

Enjoy all these new rooms as your surprise.

WHY?

Because . . . the teacher says . . . "WHY NOT?"

*When reading aloud with children, precede first line by asking children to respond, "Why?"—
each time getting softer and softer, so that at the end it is almost a whisper.

Contemplating Christmas

The Arts of Advent

The Rubens child in Mary's lap,
    Cherubic, rosy, plump,
Contrasts with Giacometti forms
    That populate the news,
So spindly, listless, sad and numb.

I am not stirred to worship him
    When swathed in purple silks,
While nations cleanse themselves in blood,
    Our youth succumb to AIDS,
And famished children dream of milk.

The Christ that gives my heart surcease,
    His Rouault eyes aflame,
Gathers in his cross-stretched arms
    The wretched of the world
And bears with them their angry pain.

The Advent candle of my life
    Burns shorter every year.
Its Rembrandt-modulated light
    Has cast a shadowed joy
Upon the season's surface cheer.

Second Thoughts on Second Coming

We light our Advent candle, Lord,
    and pray for you to come,
but not in all your glory, please,
    with thunderous roll of drum.

Come as the infant Jesus who
    has yet to know our guile,
whose strength is swathed in weakness,
    who radiates a smile.

Let us enact the Christmas tale
    adapted to our need
for holiday and merriment
    and just a touch of greed.

We fear the justice in your love
    if you return as King—
So come as baby Jesus, Lord,
    to whom we'll gladly sing.

Forgive our timid welcome as
    we struggle to believe
your Easter gift of suffering love
    that gives our fears reprieve.

The Malling of Christmas

Goblins, ghosts and wizards of the void
Are almost banished from the city mall
Before their manic dance on Halloween,
While turkeys have no economic force
Except as lures for feasting gratitude.
The lights of Christmas are already strung
And festive evergreens begin to sprout
Wherever bulging merchandise allows.

The air is sticky with soft carols crooned,
But tempo quickens as the days grow few.
Tinkling bells announce that Santa sits
Enthroned as restless children stand in line.
Displays of ribboned boxes under trees
Hold nothing but the urge to make us buy.
Do we not know the honored birthday guest
Whose party we so franticly prepare?

If we lose Christ from Christmas, we lose all
That gives expanded meaning to our gifts.
His sacrificial love begets our own.
Someday the sale of Christmas may not sell.

Pondering Christmas

Amid the mad crowd,
     elbowing its way toward
     peace on earth, goodwill,

Amid the sad crowd
     with Christmas lists too long
     and purses lean,

Amid the bad crowd,
     who slyly plunder hope
     and purchase love,

Amid the glad crowd,
     who catch the scent
     of frankincense and myrrh,

I trudge the city streets,
     needing just one face
     to share my love,

for Christmas to be real.

Amid the mad crowd, sad crowd,
     bad crowd, glad crowd,
perhaps God needs one infant face
     to cherish, name, to claim
and to reveal divine compassion
     for the world.

Outsider

Like hungry children pressed against the glass
    to see inside a crowded bright cafe
we stand outside the warm community
    from which we sense we have been turned away.

Some of us face barriers of age—
    too young, perhaps, or maybe much too old.
The pigment of our skin, our gift of race,
    may augur anguish from a world that's cold.

Many are enfeebled, blinded, deaf,
    or suffering an inward pain or grief.
Others know too much—or have too little.
    Either way can make relations brief.

Lonely, on the edge of every crowd,
    we find that everyone has been outside
and known such alienation in their life.
    In that shared knowledge we could be allied.

We need someone, despised, rejected, who
    transforms us inside out to comprehend
how, joined with God and linked with one another,
    we can achieve the world that God intends.

Spruced Up for Christmas

Twin spruce reach upward gaily in our yard,
From foot-sized seedlings into stately trees.
Twice my height, they measure years in feet,
The seasons marked by tips of tender green,
By dancing branches flashing diamond dew,
Or wrapped with dignity in ermine snow.

These spruce are quintessential Christmas trees,
No gaudy trim required for holidays.
They shimmer, nod in sturdy symmetry,
And witness to the miracle of life.
For us a symbol they cannot intend,
We see in them love's presence all year long—
Each day become a Christmas holy day.

Holy Night, Not Silent

Our sun is booming sound into the void.
It belches gaseous flares and rumbles deep
Below the narrow threshold of our ears.
Swallowed by the void, its sound is heard
By nothing sentient, we speculate.

On crisp dark nights the stars laugh
Brightly from their lofty dome,
For, lacking matter to transmit their voice,
They cackle, crackle, hiss, and boom and shriek
Wild music that we cannot regulate.

We, too, cry out into the velvet dark
Our anguish, fear, our joy, our love and praise.
Although with stars we share deaf finitude,
The universe's tumult God attends,
Whose holy listening we celebrate.

To Lenin's Tomb We Stroll

Cameras poise to snap—
"No photos," growls the guard,
"or talk. Remove your cap."
No sacred silence here;
Dead silence greets the dead.
He glows upon his bier
Beneath a focused beam.
Embalmed, his body mocks
His decomposing dream.

Nearby, St. Basil's, tall
With mounded onion domes,
Beside the Kremlin wall
Awaits rebirth, release
From age, neglect, decay.
Its dreams of Christmas peace
Return to stir the land.
      Let Lenin lie, preserved
      By artifice, as planned.
      He might awake some day,
      Not through Marxist schemes
      But by St. Basil's way.

Holy Sites

(December 25, 1999)

We sat with watchers on the shepherds' hill
     outside serenely old Jerusalem.
The craggy rocks, dark cedars and spry goats
     were starkly real on this bright Christmas day.
But angel songs no longer echoed there.

We strode the paving stones where Jesus dragged
     his cross along the *via dolorosa*
Through jeering, taunting crowds that still today
     press against those stones and blithely toss
Their plasticized detritus in the streets.

Afar, the city glows with unity;
     its cream and dark green palette soothes one's soul.
Yet possessive spires and domes of gold
     arch with musty certainty above
Each sacred site, thus fracturing the peace
     through mute cacophony's competing claims—
Like shopkeepers along the narrow lanes
     whispering, "I have a better price,"
And softly fingering their gaudy wares.

Nearby in Bethlehem armed soldiers guard
     the birthing of the Prince of Peace
For one more Christmas crowd of visitors.
     But where in all this trammeled trash and trinkets
Is the Holy One of Israel, the Christ?

Rejoice that he is risen, is not here.
     For Christ abides where hearts and minds profess
His reconciling presence in their midst.
     Such truly sacred sites are everywhere!

Joseph

Not all his neighbors' whisperings,
    nor even Mary's reticence
to share her birth of motherhood,
    nor warning words of Herod's ire
that led to furtive desert flight
    to Egypt with their threatened child,
but rearing him in Nazareth—
    that was Joseph's special trial.

With patience, pride, necessity
    he placed a saw in Jesus' hand
to follow him in carpentry.
    But even as a lad of twelve
he claimed a business alien
    to Nazareth and family.
Was Joseph shamed to have a son
    desert his craft and filial bond?

Did he, recalling Bethlehem—
    the singing silence of that night,
the strange attentiveness of stars,
    make peace at last with mystery?

Portrait Gallery

Meadowtop

The broad low-lying house seen from afar
directs its window gaze upon the sweep
of meadowland, dark-rimmed with trees and hills.
The house yields gently to the slope—a home
so much at home among tall pines,
whose fallen needles, russet soft, compose
a quiet carpet. Walking on that path,
I see up close the magic that has wrought
a unity of house and hedge and woods,
of flower, bushes, meadow grass, and stone.
Periwinkle, ferns and ivy stitch
the rooted trees securely to the earth.
The house is bedded with a quilt of blooms,
a hundred hues and fragrances drawn close.
Nothing seems amiss, but juxtaposed
precisely as a wise great love intends.
An artist, poet, nurturer of earth,
she shapes her world with exquisite finesse.
Discerning eyes suffused with grace and warmth,
a smile that crinkles all her face with joy,
a tough and tensile body, yet petite,
woman-soft and skilled in tenderness,
she is a self at home with self, with friends
and neighbors and with God, whose garden meant
to be a home for every living thing.

This poem honored on her eightieth birthday a Swiss friend, Margrit Suter, who lived in New England. It is a companion poem to "Legacy."

Constant

White hair flying like a flag of truce,
    he gathered all his facts like loyal troops
assembled at attention rank on rank
    while leaders met, signed papers and shook hands.

Not a soldier nor a general, he,
    but quartermaster of the day's details,
without whose duty to both need and truth
    few wars are won or life made history.

Work colleague in the Office of Research of the National Council of the Churches of Christ in the U.S.A., Constant Jacquet was editor of the *Yearbook of American and Canadian Churches* until his death in 1990. This is a memorial poem.

No Kidding

When the phone rings,
　　I answer with delight.
When the door sounds,
　　I open it outright.

When my boss asks,
　　I'm quick to do my part.
When a need calls,
　　I offer it my heart.

If the church needs
　　Help to aid its weak,
Disabled folk, then I
　　Provide what churches seek.

If a camper wants
　　To learn about the skies,
I plan a study guide,
　　For I'm considered wise.

If the future's joy
　　From staff colleagues is hid,
I bring them merriment,
　　'cause really Ima Kidd!

Ima Jean Kidd was a staff colleague in the National Council of Churches of Christ in the U.S.A. until her 1989 retirement from a position that encompassed church camping and advocacy for the disabled.

AVE of NRSV

Lover of Scripture,
Respecter of Words.

    The resonant gift of his singing
    Delights and enchants those who hear—
        A musical missionary
        Voicing the Word with his song
        And giving his heart's joy release.

Lover of Scripture,
Respecter of Words.

    He is attuned to this calling,
    A calling that sings in his ear—
        A marketing missionary
        Believing the strength of the Word
        To woo the whole world to God's peace.

Arthur Van Eck (AVE) was retiring from staff for the New Revised Standard Version (NRSV) of the Bible Translation Committee, National Council of Churches, when this was written.

A Lexicon for Martin

When I just close my eyes
And think your name,
My inner eye sees "kindness."
You—a world-spanning, computer-toting
Telecommunicator, jawing with journalists
Who'd gladly shred anybody's dignity
For a headline—
KIND?

Try again. My inner ear
Hears "calm."
You—who first receive
The hushed bad news behind closed doors,
Or panic-driven on a shrieking telephone,
Or borne upon a tidal wave
That crashes on your shore—
CALM?

Another word appears
Upon my inward screen: "loyalty."
You—who know enough to blackmail
All your enemies—and nearly half your friends,
Who could be cynical and tough,
Calculating, coarse or simply sad—
A man to
TRUST?

Once more I listen
To an inner voice that whispers "wisdom."
You—grasping for the tumbleweed of facts,
The evanescent play of light and shade
We label "truth,"
The rounded mouthings of "official" speech—
How can you be so
WISE?

Suddenly, more words conjoin
In fanciful collage,
Delineating you in sharp detail:
A man of FAITH,
Whose kindness imitates eternal love,
Whose calm rests firmly on his Christian hope,
Whose trust extends because it is received,
Whose wisdom seeks the purposes of God.

Yes, that *is* Martin Bailey!

A Bit of Baileyhoo

Martin went to Moscow
    When relationships were frigid.
He took a trip to Cuba
    When restrictions there were rigid.

He flew to Nicaragua
    And to poor El Salvador.
He visited and filmed them
    In spite of a hot war.

To the Middle East he fluttered
    Like a moth into a flame,
To South Africa, Korea—
    Danger is his middle name.

He looked and learned and listened,
    Then often wrote a book.
Each trip was worth a story,
    But, oh—the chances that he took!

He visited fine places,
    Though the timing was not best.
Just as I suspected,
    He grew up in the Midwest!

This lighthearted poem and "A Lexicon for Martin" honored at his retirement Martin Bailey, communications officer for the United Church of Christ and later for the National Council of Churches of Christ in the U.S.A.

Stage Directions

Clamp a cigar between his teeth
　And he could mingle
　　With politicos
　　　In any smoke-filled room.

Straighten his tie and press his suit,
　He could talk big deals
　　With C.E.O.'s
　　　Of any corporation.

Give him a badge and gun,
　He could tell anyone
　　Where to go,
　　　Including jail.

With notebook, press card, pen,
　He could track down
　　Corruption
　　　Wherever it occurs.

Set him before a college class,
　He could discourse
　　Like Socrates
　　　On any theme.

Put a collar round his neck,
　And it might chafe a bit
　　As he dreams dreams and
　　　Walks his talk.

Capable of playing many roles
　For truth and justice,
　　He takes his cues
　　　From faithful hope and love.

This poem honors Charles Rawlings, urban minister extraordinaire and colleague in the National Council of Churches.

The Astronomy of Colleagues

Some of us are stars—
>Brilliant, cool, remote,

While many, blazing suns,
>Envelop us in warmth,

Or streak across our path
>Like comets.

Just a few have grace
>To be a moon—

Reflecting others' light,
>Blessing us

Especially in times
>Of darkness.

Dedicated to Robert Polk, who served as an interim division director at a difficult transition time in the National Council of Churches, 1997.

A Lesson in the Arts

When novice artists try to sketch a horse,
    they need a model—real-life, photo or
    another artist's work.

One knows a horse until the pencil balks—
    as parts to whole become a bit confused,
    details are blurred or vague.

A horse recalled is equine, to be sure,
    but minor gaps in observation may
    create an awkward mare.

When poems sketch a friend, the pencil halts—
    as marker of a mystery,
    of private personhood.

I can remark her virtues, humor, skills
    of handling people, budgets and
    complex bureaucracies.

But when my pencil probes her spirit's dreams,
    just shadows flicker
    from her ecstasies.

Affection and respect restrain my words,
    lest what I cannot comprehend
    distort the savage beauty of her self.

This poem honors Roman Catholic nun Dorothy Savage, colleague in the National Council of Churches and avid student of spirituality.

Iconography

How shall I remember Olga—
    as a flame that flares
    with tongue of fire,
        or smoldering coals
        hot with energy?

I'll keep an icon in my mind:
    The penumbra of her hair
    haloing her face
        as she embraces me
        with her warm smile.

With Olga everyone's a "ten"
    until some foolish soul
    ignites her wrath
        and tumbles to a "one"—
        or turns to ash.

Her work is orderly and quick,
    but in her heart
    a vast disorder reigns,
        for she has let in
        everyone she meets.

This siren Greek brings joy and gaiety;
    so laugh, rejoice
    and do not weep
        when she departs,
        for we go with her
        in her heart.

This poem honors Olga Paspalas, my secretary in Professional Church Leadership, National Council of Churches, upon her retirement in 1996.

Summative Evaluation

A spiritual calculus
Counts the folk who fill the pews
Sunday by Sunday, week by week—
A decade of such reckoning:

How do you weigh the presence
Of one, eyes creased by cancer's pain,
Who lifts her head in steadfast praise?
Or another, shuffling with arthritic dignity
Into a favored seat?

How calculate the widower
Who slowly learns again to smile,
The tentative young man brought
By a shy but beaming maid?

Is there a special number
For the brusque, the bristly, bored, or bruised—
Who also come again?
Or the devout, who skim a tattered Bible
As the Word is shared?

A pastor glances with an anxious eye
At vacant seats,
Seeing not the emptiness
But the person missed.

God takes our sum of ministry
And reckons it mysteriously,
Until our pride and our despair
Become our energy and hope.

A decade of the ministry of Presbyterian pastor Stephen H. Phelps is the source of this poem.

Haiku for Kosuke Koyama

Smiling East-West spirit,
You move with sun and Son,
Shining peace on us.

Like a child piling blocks
Your words construct new dreams,
towering poet.

Gentle and strong, as trees
Bend gracefully in wind,
you stand—and I bow.

These three Japanese-style seventeen-syllable poems were written to honor retiring Professor of Ecumenics, Dr. Kosuke Koyama, of Union Theological Seminary in New York City, May 1996.

Deep Waters

Mourning with Those Who Mourn

Blessed are those who mourn
With those who newly mourn,
Who bear their helpless rage,
Who bring a gift of grief,
Whose anger ignites hope
Against injustices.

In lonely depths of loss
One's throat constricts with pain,
As fingers of despair
Choke an aching hope.
Shared grief begins release
As sobs tear loose fresh breath.

The gift of grief is blest
When it becomes God's rod
And staff that comfort us,
God's ever-present help
In time of greatest need.
Blessed are those who mourn.

Legacy

Our friend lies dying in her bed,
As strange adventures loom ahead.

While tears of mine fall on her sheet,
I know she dreams of whom she'll meet.

She has no fear except for us,
As we await her exodus.

I'd like to take her by the hand
As she departs her cherished land

And lead her with a tender heart—
Except I don't know where to start.

If friendship can sustain her now,
Her orphans take that solemn vow.

This leave-taking, despite her pain,
Is in her loving hands again,

As she remembers garden seeds
To share, among our other needs,

And plans decided in the past
To will her treasures so they'll last.

Her legacy of love and hope
Extends beyond most human scope,

For when she slips along that way
We cannot walk—or make her stay,

We'll know God blessed a garden space
To welcome her with special grace.

The Killing Frost

Autumn branches burn with flaming leaves
like smudge-pots for our garden on the hill.
The valley, with false blankets of chill cloud,
is first to lose the harvest that remains,
while on our daring slopes we celebrate
a few more precious weeks of gold and rust.
But winter's penalty we'll then await—
To pay in blizzard for deferring frost.

The killing frost is fickle as it bursts
the tender cells of blossoms, leaves and stems.
Some marigolds stand firm while others die.
Snapdragons, pansies and geraniums
outlast the sturdy zinnia and chives.
Snap beans, tomatoes and fat squash succumb
while gentle lettuce and lean leeks survive.
They yield no simple rule for my green thumb!

With people, too, no rule seems to apply.
The kindest, dearest or most beautiful,
intelligent, self-giving, strong and brave
seem not to weather human killing frosts
with longer days, exempted by their worth.
Forgive us, God, we cannot understand
why wisdom, love and goodness on this earth
are not protected high ground like the land.

Graveyard Humor

I have haunted graveyards recently—
    A Hempstead English churchyard dank with moss,
      its tombstones cracked
      and heaved by centuries
        of nature's cold
          benign neglect.

    A village cemetery in Vermont,
      whose sturdy English forebears
      may have kin
        in Hempstead plots.

    A lovely Massachusetts green,
      gently tended, spare,
      its fresh mounds mowed
        and sunken graves trimmed, too.

I have roamed each graveyard, row on row,
    listening for clues
    of what transpires
      among the dead.

    A silence like the hush
      when music stops
      before applause
        (or is it just before
        the concert starts?)
      throbs among these stones.
Is this the end—or a beginning?

There is an emptiness, an absence here,
    despite our pitiful attempts,
      midst broken stones,
      eroded names and dates,
to preserve and recollect.

The graveyard mocks our efforts. It implies
    another meaning to
      "Here, lies . . ."

Circling Back to Campus

The trees are taller now, their trunks more stalwart and secure.
Buildings made by human hands have worn and crumbled some,
While bold new structures, giving shape to bolder dreams, appear.
Waters flow in patterns, where the changeless rocks abide.

    The familiar here is cherished,
        the new, ambivalently welcomed,
        the broken or torn down, mourned.

    Each turning on the path stirs memory:
        We fought for racial openness—and won.
        Looking to these hills, we prayed for light.
        And here—a budding love that never bloomed.
        There, where earnest talking molded lives.

    The rippling creek still sings its endless tunes.
        Our fingers touch, electric, warm and sure.
        We link arms with each other, with the past.
        For this is who we know we were—and are.

An Office Stonehenge

Stone gray and moss green steel,
    the filing cabinets,
    like battered monoliths,
        stand apart
        in grave neglect.

The light shines dimly on the folders
    stacked on edge inside.
    Bent tabs, once fingered urgently,
        convey their cryptic news
        of secrets hid within.

The papers hallowed there in creamy folds
    tease my reluctant memory
    of earnest work—that seems as flat
        as paper now, compressed
        in compact bins.

Ten years of yellowed time fade
    and mock the dailiness
    of conscientious work
        that blinked upon my screen
        in emerald concentration.

Connected then like keys
    to power source, I feel unplugged,
    remote. I struggle to reclaim
        validity and sense
        for those brave hours.

Someday these records may no longer
    simply be outdated
    by today's immediacy,
        like runes whose glyphs
        do not communicate.

When might the magic moment come
    when they transmute into
    the fossils of a treasured chronicle—
        a link with God's eternity,
        a word from our collective past?

The Mortal Mover

Packing boxes line my barren hall,
Each carton gagged with sticky, tough wide tape,
My life enclosed, compressed and sorted, sealed.
That part of me that can be caged and shelved,
Domesticated, scrutinized and boxed
Will soon unfold, shake loose from newsprint wrap
And grow accustomed to another space.

Moving is a time to lighten loads.
The files and drawers, closets, storage bins
Have all been culled of only second best.
Ruthlessly discarding from my past
Those tatters that can jar my memory,
I bravely say, "One can't keep everything,"
While knowing it is life to which I cling.

Like snakes that shed their skin before they grow,
I've moved, discarded, moved a dozen times
But feel diminished each successive step.
The more I move the more I leave behind;
So few of family and friends remain who know
The "me" as child, as youth, mature adult.
Each move seems one more certain step toward death.

But, cartons emptied, set aside at last,
I'm liberated to explore the new,
And life expands, enlarges, is enriched
By all the stimuli the move portends.
And yet I hope that someone keeps account,
Recalls what I reluctantly let go.
God knows that I have tried to stay intact.
God knows. Yes—that's my hope. God knows.

Memory

The moment shimmers sharp and crisp—
    The sun's bright window warmth,
    The air-conditioned drone now sliced
        By high-pitched distant talk—
Breakfasted, relaxed and savoring
    Night's curve of bodies nestled
        In the certainty of love,
I wonder:
    How could I forget this instant's joy?
Yet one day I'll reflect through clouded mind—
    Was that in Albany, Great Falls, or Santa Fe?
    July or August, June, or lovely May?
Each day blends in an ecstasy of life.

Memory can sicken if love sours,
Can blunt responsibility, numb pain.
It muddles or conflates selectively
What one knew then—and what one knows today.
The truth of memory refines itself
When intermingled with some others' past
As recollected through their consciousness.

Lord, open me to humble clarity
To learn in whole what I have known in part.
Help me remember with deep gratitude
    The essence of things worthy of recall,
    The kindliness of some forgetfulness,
    The faith that you remember me complete,
        Should I be lost in memory's retreat.

Afterglows

We often visit sunsets now
    and marvel at the rapid slip
    of flaming disc below earth's rim,
        viewed bravely through the evening haze—
    a billion motes of daily dust.

Surrounded by the afterglow,
    we trace that final steady march
    of sun across the silent sky.
Sometimes we parse the equinox
    as sun sets left or right of hills—
    a simple syntax, earthly speech.

Our lives have lovely sunsets, too—
    those solemn moments when we note
    the setting down, the letting go,
        and stare into those vivid fires
    of energy through memory.

From friends' farewells and honors we
    take courage for the deepened dusk
    and rest beneath assembling stars.
Beyond the quiet comes the dawn,
    a lightened sky, a rising wind,
    a quickened pulse, a clearer eye.

Renewed, refreshed, we reach once more
    to claim new tasks, to stretch toward goals,
    to let the needs of others drain
        our spirits and our energy,
        to hope, to love, to laugh, to play.

Though sunsets grieve the death of days,
    consuming, cleansing holy pyres
    that mark the evening's closing hour,
we live not only daily grief
    but also dawn, as each new morn
    prepares for resurrection day.

The Vanity of Vanity

I stand upon the shore of life
And feel the undertow of emptiness
For nothing lasts. Sand castles wash away.
Debris of life, like empty shells,
Drifts out again to sea
In restless ebb and flow.
The traces of my life
Will disappear beneath the dunes,
Or, snared among sea grass,
Will eddy aimlessly like flotsam
In the waves of history.

To think we daily strive in vain
For any recognition after death
Is fearful, wry, and tempting comfort:
>   Cease trying to protect your name,
>   Engrave it on the future's memory.
>   Posterity itself will surely die
>   And speak your honored, precious name
>   No more.

Am I, are you, mere dust?
Or sand, or shells, or scattering of bones?
If we are dust,
It is the dust of stars.
We are God's cosmic creatures
In a universe so vast
The mind of God alone can span.

Is it enough to know that God—
In love—intended our existence?
Does this assure our immortality?

I do not know,
But I would rather die in faith
That Jesus is a true interpreter—
>   And never learn in death
>   That he was wrong—
Than live in certainty that life is vain
And therefore never fully live at all.

Gazing at the Sun

A Paean

To My Beloved on His Seventieth Birthday

Beneath the surface of my daily acts
      like cooking, writing, paying bills, my heart
      proclaims each day remarkable because:

The rushing current of your energy
      sweeps me along its churning riverbed
      and I am drawn into its urgent swirl.

You spend yourself in reckless bankruptcy
      for God, for others, for your family,
      replenished daily by your loyalty.

The fan of wrinkles from your eyes and cheeks
      spreads kindly smiles upon the wary world
      and still reserves its warmest ones for me.

Your questions burrow social interchange
      with probing thought and excavate a mound
      of insight, humor, lively new ideas.

You live in music as it lives in you.
      A whistle is your clever mimicry,
      and loving arms your instrument of choice.

Your body speaks its joy and love of life—
      its loping stride and punctuating head,
      or lithe physique sunk deep into a chair.

Your avid conversation with the world—
      through letters, books, electric circuitry—
      engages and connects me with it, too.

This reckoning of riches floods my days
      with gratitude for life you bring to me.
      I celebrate and cherish who you are.

A Breakfast Blessing

Beloved, when the bed springs softly creak,
as you slide warm bare feet
onto cold floor,

While I am nestled deep within the sheets,
and hear the coffee mill
obey your touch,

As water flows, doors open, close, and you
are spreading marmalade or
peeling fruit,

My dreams evaporate and bedclothes cool.
I stretch, breathe in another
precious day,

Praise God in joyful daily gratitude
for loyal love—the miracle
of you.

42nd Wedding Anniversary Poem, 1995

Farewell, My Love

We linger with our fingers interlocked
Until propriety requires decisive break.
      Doors close and engines roar.
      Footfalls retreat.
      A wave, forced smiles.
      Eyes front to face our separate worlds.
Communion now is simply memory.
      These little deaths.
I take no comfort that they practice
For the permanent farewell.

Words muttered to myself alone
Drift like tufts of dust beneath our bed.
The thoughts I wish to share with you each hour
Clutter like today's unopened mail.
What use is it repeatedly
      To weigh the emptiness of space together filled,
      To sense a bed grown cavernous and cold,
      To taste the supper silence, bland and dry?
Such knowledge I protest!

Created incomplete, I have grown whole
      Savoring your love.
Why must I practice for the day
When life is sundered, torn in half?
      God, take me swiftly
      Should I, crippled,
      Need to lean on Thee alone.

Perspective

Alone on our hillside I see
    green drain from stiff grass into the soil,
    trees bloodied at their tips, raking a steel sky,
    September zinnias and marigolds, bursting with final bloom
        in desperate gaiety,
    gardens heavy with harvest, leaves yellowing, drooped and
        parched, fruit swelling with seed,
    nectar-greedy bees, imperious cicadas, aimless butterflies,
        lethargic flies—
    all choking in a claustrophobic haze of fading hills and
        throbbing night,
    as cold stars stare aloof.

Beside you
    the milky warmth of summer nourishes our privacy,
    the flame of leaves promises a cozy hearth;
    chrysanthemums and bold gazanias bloom with wild abandon,
    zinnias thrust fresh faces from their tattered foliage,
    sturdy geraniums glow a startling red that stirs my blood.
    insects pulse in camaraderie,
        as stars sign their silent benediction.

I am dizzy with delight,
    gluttonous with warm fruit,
        drunk with the ferment of harvest.

The difference, love,
    is you.

Testament

Breathing the humid dust of history
  in the seminary's rare book room,
  we stood hush-voiced.

A small thick book,
  barely three-inch square,
  its binding stiff as old men's knees,
  leather darkly aged,
   passed from hand
   to trembling hand.

It was a Hebrew testament,
  valued for itself,
  but also for the hand
  that penned the faded words:
   "My wife's book and mine—
   Robert Browning."

Three possessives in a single phrase,
  this love-laden book
  momentarily weighed upon my palm.
  Then, silently, I pressed
   the sacred book
   into the hands of my beloved,
    my own inscription written in my eyes.

This volume is among many other rare treasures in the library of Jewish Theological Seminary in New York City.

Marriage Bounds

"I may be going blind!" she cries.
"My love, then let me be your eyes."
    "My ears are growing dim," he fears.
    "Beloved, let me be your ears."

Love gives us life, keeps no accounts,
No careful measure ounce for ounce
    To get what we deserve and so
    To give in justice what we owe.

Give justice, yes, but move beyond
To love whose bounty knows no bound,
    For marriages, if truly blest,
    To God's unmeasured love attest.

I Cannot Bear to Look upon My Love

I cannot bear to look upon my love
    For it would be like gazing at the sun
Or gathering the treasures of the earth
    Into a glittering heap of diamonds,
Of gold and coin of every distant realm.
    Better that I bring the interest,
My daily sum from that great treasure store.
    Were I to draw it out in one big draft
You could not spend it, fathom its true worth.

Like sorcery, the magic of my love
    Replenishes, as check on check on check—
A hundred bucketsful—cannot exhaust
    That fervent, overflowing wild supply
Which grows in quality as it depletes.
    I will die richer in my love for you
Than I can spend in all my years of love,
    So take my daily sum and squander it
With me—in joy!